See What I Mean?

See What I Mean?

See the change
we can be in the world

Real life stories
by the author of *Plan Be*

Dave Andrews

Authentic

Copyright © 2010 Dave Andrews

16 15 14 13 12 11 10   7 6 5 4 3 2 1

First published 2010 by Authentic Media Limited
Milton Keynes
www.authenticmedia.co.uk

British Library Cataloguing in Publication Data
A catalogue record for this book is available from the British Library

ISBN-13: 978-1-85078-847-8

Cover design by Paul Airy, Four-Nine-ZeroDesign
(www.fourninezerodesign.co.uk)
Printed and bound in the UK by J. F. Print Ltd., Sparkford, Somerset

Contents

Contents

Preface

Like most Christians, I have always related to Jesus as a saviour.

I've seen more than my fair share of miraculous transformation in people's lives. Yet it seems to me that, on the whole, things aren't getting better - they're getting worse. In spite of our illusions of progress, more than one hundred and twenty million people were killed in wars during the twentieth century. That's more than all the people killed in all the wars fought in all the previous twenty centuries put together.

We seem to be unwilling - or unable - to save ourselves. So, without a saviour of some kind, I don't have much hope for the planet.

But my understanding of how Jesus can save us is always changing.

As a toddler I related to Jesus as a relative.

My parents were pious people. My father was a pastor and my mother was part of the ministry too. We were a close family, and my parents talked to us about Jesus as if he were a member of our family.

I don't recall seeing Jesus at our home. But Dad and Mum told us all about him. Each night before we went to sleep they'd read us a story about him and show us pictures of him from an old storybook. I can still see those pictures of Jesus. There was one of him carrying a lamb he'd found on his shoulders. And there was another of him sitting with some kids – that was my favourite, because the kid on his knee looked a lot like me!

As a child I related to Jesus as a friend.

When my parents emigrated from England to Australia when I was eight years old I was uprooted from the only place that I knew. And I was separated from all the relatives I loved – all of them except Jesus. When we were coming over on the boat, someone played 'Somewhere over the Rainbow' when we crossed the equator. But the antipodes proved to be anything but the magical Land of Oz for me.

It was uncool to wear shoes to school. And trying to run around the playground in the midday sun – on blistering-hot rock-hard bitumen – on my little, pink, soft bare feet – was torture. To make matters worse, at that time in Australia it was a crime to have a posh English accent – and I was beaten unmercifully for being a 'smartmouthed pommie bastard'. Often I felt that Jesus was the only friend that I had in the world.

As an adolescent I related to Jesus as a hero.

When I read the Gospels, I saw Jesus in a whole new light. He struck me as a man's man. He said what he meant and meant what he said. He believed in love and justice and stood up bravely for his beliefs. So Jesus became my role model. And I took every chance I could to 'be like Jesus' and 'do a Jesus'.

There was a little kid in our neighbourhood who everybody thought was a few sandwiches short of a picnic. All the kids used to pick on him; but there was one big kid in particular who used to pick on him a lot.

'What would Jesus do?' I asked myself. 'He'd lay his body on the line to stop the poor blighter from being bullied,' I told myself. So I vowed that the next time I saw him being attacked, I'd intervene. As it turned out, when I did step in I got beaten to a pulp and had to be rushed off to hospital. But my bruises only served to strengthen my admiration for the man who laid down his life for his friends.

As an adult I have always related to Jesus as a guru.

I went to university in the sixties, when revolution was all the rage. And I agreed with much of Marx's analysis of society. But I thought the solutions to problems Christ proposed were far more radical than Marx.

In the seventies I went to India, along with the rest of my generation. I studied Krishna, Moses, Buddha, and Mohammed. Much of what they said was the truth. But, to me, Christ was the truth of which they spoke.

So I have spent most of my life setting up intentional, multicultural, inter-religious communities based on the uniquely radical, outrageously inclusive, non-violent principles of the Rabbi from Nazareth. And, at present, my family and I are part of an inner-city network called the Waiters Union, which is committed to developing a discipleship community with disadvantaged groups of people in our home town.

Since the publication of *Plan Be* many people have asked me to share stories from my own life that show what I mean. They've asked to see how I seek to embody the Be-Attitudes and try to be the change we want to see in the world.

Most of the stories here are drawn from material I have used in other books, and I am very grateful for the permission of the publishers of *Christi-Anarchy, Not Religion but Love, A Divine Society* and *Building a Better World* to use edited excerpts from these books in this publication.

Dave Andrews
Brisbane 2009

I believe that what Jesus taught us in the Sermon on the Mount about the way we ought to live is the only way we can save ourselves from destroying ourselves. Indeed, Jesus says that if we do not practice the Be-Attitudes we will destroy not only ourselves, but also those who are closest to us.

> Therefore everyone who hears these words of mine and puts them into practice is like a wise person who built his house on the rock. The rain came down, the streams rose, and the winds blew and beat against that house; yet it did not fall, because it had its foundation on the rock. But everyone who hears these words of mine and does not put them into practice is like a foolish man who built his house on sand. The rain came down, the streams rose, and the winds blew and beat against that house, and it fell with a great crash. (Matt. 7:24-27)

Just so we get the point of Jesus' parable clearly, we need to note that he is using classic Jewish parallelism to compare and contrast two completely different positive and negative scenarios.

Positive Scenario	Negative Scenario
Those who hear his words and put them into practice	Those who hear his words and do not put them into practice
Are like a person who builds a house on rock	Are like a person who builds a house on sand
Their house will be able to withstand the storms	Their house will not be able to withstand the storms It will collapse 'with a great crash'

Jesus is saying that those who put his words into practice and embody the spirit of the Be-Attitudes will be building their 'houses' on such solid foundations they will be able to cope with all the difficulties they will have to face in life.

But those who hear and speak his words yet do not put them into practice – who do not embody the spirit of the Be-Attitudes – will be building their 'houses' for their families and communities on such faulty foundations they will not be able to cope with the stresses and strains of life. They will 'crash'.

I'm told that the Greek words for 'great crash' could be better translated 'mass burial'. And so what Jesus is actually saying is that those who do not seek to embody the Be-Attitudes will not only not be able to cope with the stresses and strains of life but when they crash (as they eventually will), they will take all those closest to them down with them.

So the only way we can build a better world and save ourselves from destroying ourselves and those closest to us is to practice the Be-Attitudes.

I believe, therefore, in the Be-Attitudes celebrated in the Beatitudes.

> Blessed are the poor in spirit,
> for theirs is the kingdom of heaven.
> Blessed are those who mourn,
> for they will be comforted.
> Blessed are the meek,
> for they will inherit the earth.
> Blessed are those who hunger and thirst
> for righteousness,
> for they will be filled.
> Blessed are the merciful,
> for they will be shown mercy.
> Blessed are the pure in heart,
> for they will see God.
> Blessed are the peacemakers,
> for they will be called children of God.
> Blessed are those who are persecuted
> because of righteousness,
> for theirs is the kingdom of heaven.
>
> (Matthew 5:1-10)

I seek to live by the Be-Attitudes I believe in by being a person who identifies with the poor in spirit; who grieves over injustice in the world; who gets angry but not aggressive; who seeks to do justice even to my enemies; who extends compassion to all those in need; who acts with integrity; who works for peace in the midst of the violence; and who suffers myself, rather than inflicting suffering on others.

**We can be people
who are with the
poor in spirit**
and who see the
difference it makes to
the way we locate
ourselves in the world.

When I was younger and read 'Blessed are you poor, for yours is the kingdom of God' (Luke 6:20) I used to rejoice, because I thought I was poor and Jesus promised the kingdom of God to poor people like me.

I remember as a young man reading the parable Jesus told about the rich man (traditionally called Dives) and the poor man Lazarus - and cheering. I was a poor student whose parents could not afford to pay for me to go to university (I only was able to go to university because I got a scholarship 'funded from the scraps that fell from the rich man's table'). The only person in the story I felt I could identify with was the poor man, Lazarus. And, the way I read the story, although Dives gave Lazarus a hard time Lazarus eventually triumphed over Dives. God would make sure that all of us who were poor would win - and the rich would lose - in the end.

After all, the story went like this:

> There was a rich man (Dives) who was dressed in purple and fine linen and lived in luxury every day. At his gate was laid a beggar named Lazarus, covered with sores and longing to eat what fell from the rich man's table. Even the dogs came and licked his sores. The beggar died and the angels carried him to Abraham's side. The rich man also died and was buried. In hell, where he was in torment, he looked up and saw Abraham far away, with Lazarus by his side. So he called to him, 'Father Abraham, have pity on me and send Lazarus to dip the tip of his finger in water and

cool my tongue, because I am in agony in this fire.'
But Abraham replied, 'Son, remember in your
lifetime you received your good things, while
Lazarus received bad things, but now he is
comforted here and you are in agony.' (Luke
16:19-25)

As a student at university, however, I came to realize that
there were many people in the world who were a lot poorer
than I was. I was introduced to the concepts of 'relative'
poverty and 'absolute' poverty. I learned that people in
relative poverty do not have as much as others do, while
those in absolute poverty do not have enough to even
survive. And I learned that there were millions of people
in Australia who were relatively poor and more than a
billion people in the world who were absolutely poor.

In trying to grasp the concept that a billion people in the
world were absolutely poor I visualized 1,000,000,000
hungry neighbours standing in single file outside my flat,
empty bowls in hand, begging for food. And I calculated
that if all my hungry neighbours stood in single file outside
my flat, one metre apart, the line would be so long that it
would stretch down the road, across town, and wrap
round the world more than twenty-five times. And then I
figured out that if I jumped in the Morris Mini-Minor I had
at the time and drove down the line at the local speed limit
(60 kilometres per hour), day and night, week after week,
month after month, without a break, it would take me two
and a half years to reach the end of the line.

I could not get the line of hungry neighbours standing outside my flat out of my mind. And I couldn't help but wonder what life was like for those of my neighbours who found themselves standing at the end of the line. So when I had the chance to check out what life was really like at the end of the line, I moved to India and got involved with people living in one of the poorest slums in Asia.

• • •

The Kanjars were a tribe of a thousand people who migrated to New Delhi in search of food during a time of famine and ended up eking out an existence ever since in one of the city's slums.

It was a very precarious existence. A thousand people lived in two hundred little huts with thatched roofs supported by bamboo poles that consistently failed to keep out inclement weather - the cold in winter, the heat in summer, the rain in monsoon. Each hut housed a family of five or more - one or more grandparents, a couple of parents, and two or three children in the space of a tent fit for two - it was a tight squeeze.

Around the huts the dusty ground was covered with bits of trash, different kinds of refuse, and faeces. Pigs rooted through the rubbish, searching for titbits of excrement to snaffle.

Their only water source was a smelly, stagnant pool nearby. It bred mosquitoes that carried malaria around the settlement. There wasn't a single tap or pump to supply drinking water. If people wanted a drink, they had to beg for it.

The Kanjars tried to survive on a diet of rotten fruit and vegetables that they scavenged from the waste bins in the neighbourhood. Disease was rampant. Death stalked the encampment. There were so many deaths that I think at least once a week one of the families in the slum lost a loved one.

The people lived with tremendous dignity. But behind the smiles there were always tears. The joke was always on them. They were outcaste, illiterate, illegal squatters, always being hassled by the public and harassed by the police.

When my friends and I began to visit the Kanjars they were very suspicious. They had no visitors who were friends. There was no one who just wanted to spend time with them, relate to them, talk with them, listen to them, or struggle with their concerns in an open-ended manner.

The only visitors who ever made their way to the slums were politicians who came looking for votes at election time or proselytizers who came looking for souls to convert to their particular sect. But no one ever stayed.

The Kanjars said they felt abandoned by everybody – including God. In fact, they called themselves 'God-forsaken people'. Because they did not have work to earn money to buy food for their families they had to scavenge for scraps from the dumps. The scraps from the dumps were often dirty and gave their children diarrhoea, and when they got diarrhoea they got dehydrated. They didn't have access to potable drinking water to re-hydrate the sick children and couldn't afford to buy the medicine they needed. They cried out to God to save their children – but he never did, and these children died in their arms.

Job may have had in mind the plight of people just like the Kanjars when he wrote, 'Along the city streets, the wounded and dying cry out, yet God does nothing' (Job 24:12). For the Kanjars, at the end of the line there is only death.

• • •

After one of my visits to the slum I remember reflecting on the parable about the rich man Dives and the poor man Lazarus again – and screaming.

Because, in that context – meeting people who were literally 'covered in sores', who longed 'to eat the scraps from the rich man's table' – the only person in the story I felt I could identify with was the rich man, Dives. And the way I read the story, though Lazarus, the poor man, had a really hard time, in the end God vindicated him. While Dives, the rich man – like me – was doomed.

After all, the story went like this:

> There was a rich man (Dives) who was dressed in purple and fine linen and lived in luxury every day. At his gate was laid a beggar named Lazarus, covered with sores and longing to eat what fell from the rich man's table. Even the dogs came and licked his sores. The beggar died and the angels carried him to Abraham's side. The rich man also died and was buried. In hell, where he was in torment, he looked up and saw Abraham far away, with Lazarus by his side. So he called to

him, 'Father Abraham, have pity on me and send
Lazarus to dip the tip of his finger in water and
cool my tongue, because I am in agony in this fire.'
But Abraham replied, 'Son, remember in your
lifetime you received your good things, while
Lazarus received bad things, but now he is
comforted here and you are in agony.'
(Luke 16:19-25)

Jesus is very clear that, as far as he is concerned, the only
hope there is for people like Dives is for us to acknowledge
that we are rich, but choose to identify ourselves with poor
people, like Lazarus.

The great example in the Gospels of one who was rich like
Dives but who chose to identify himself with the poor was
Zacchaeus.

Jesus entered Jericho and was passing through. A
man was there by the name of Zacchaeus; he was
a chief tax collector and was wealthy. He wanted
to see who Jesus was, but being a short man he
could not, because of the crowd. So he ran ahead
and climbed a sycamore-fig tree to see him, since
Jesus was coming that way.

When Jesus reached the spot, he looked up and
said to him, 'Zacchaeus, come down immediately.
I must stay at your house today.' So he came down
at once and welcomed him gladly.

All the people saw this and began to mutter, 'He
has gone to be the guest of a "sinner."'

> But Zacchaeus stood up and said to the Lord, 'Look, Lord! Here and now I give half of my possessions to the poor, and if I have cheated anybody out of anything, I will pay back four times the amount.' Jesus said to him, 'Today salvation has come to this house, because this man, too, is a son of Abraham. For the Son of Man came to seek and to save what was lost.' (Luke 19:1-10)

In many ways the story of Zacchaeus is the counterpoint to the story of Dives. Both Zacchaeus and Dives were rich. Both Zacchaeus and Dives showed contempt for the poor: Zacchaeus by robbing them blind; and Dives by turning a blind eye to the misery around about him and living a life of shameless luxury. But one day Zacchaeus met Jesus. Zacchaeus 'came down', sat with Jesus who sat with the poor, and as a result of their conversation he promised 'to give half of (his) possessions to the poor' and 'pay back four times' the amount of whatever he had stolen from anyone. And, as a consequence of his choice to identify with the poor in spirit, Jesus said, 'salvation has come to this house'.

So I realized that if I acknowledged I was rich like Dives but wanted to choose to identify myself with the poor in spirit, then I needed to do what Zacchaeus had done. I needed to come down to earth, sit with Jesus who sits with the poor, share my possessions with the poor, and make restitution to any people I may have ripped off – either intentionally or unintentionally.

• • •

Ange and I started with 'sharing our possessions with the poor'. We read the story about Jesus saying to a rich young person like us: 'Sell everything you have and give to the poor . . . then come, follow me' (Luke18:22). Because we hadn't been to seminary, we didn't know it could be interpreted to mean other than what it actually said. So because that is what we thought Jesus wanted us to do, that is what we did. We sold our house, and everything we possessed, and we put all the money into a trust to fund the work that we did with the poor in India.

In the slums of India, 'coming down to earth' for me meant sitting with the people on *charpois*, in the midst of the squalor, eating pieces of *chapatti* and drinking cups of *chai*, dipping the hardened bread in the hot tea to soften it so we could chew on it while we talked about their concerns for their community.

What the Kanjars had lost in terms of their dignity they more than made up for in guts. Their struggle against seemingly overwhelming odds was fought with lots of courage and lots of laughter. We were encouraged and strengthened by their infectious style of heroism and sense of humour. They may have been demoralized, but they taught us valuable lessons about the morality of survival.

As our friendships deepened, we learned from them not only the art of survival in an urban slum, but we also began to feel the anguish they felt in their struggle to survive. As we discussed the issues they had to face every day of their lives, we decided to work with them to see if together we could find some long-term solutions that would minimize the anguish associated with their struggle for survival and also increase their chances of surviving.

In the slums of India, 'sitting with Jesus who sits with the poor' for me meant being sensitive to the fact that, whether they knew it or not, Jesus related to the Kanjars as family. As far as Jesus was concerned, 'whatever we did to the least of these, his little brothers and sisters, we did it to him' (Matt. 25:40). Thus we needed to be always sensitive to what Jesus would want for his family.

Time went by and week after week, month after month, year after year, we worked on a whole range of problems together - everything from getting a regular water supply to improving nutrition and sanitation. We solved each problem together - on the basis of what they wanted and what we sensed Jesus wanted for his family. We all agreed that the most important thing was saving the children in the community from dying prematurely.

But we all knew there was no quick fix for the Kanjars. The only hope they had was to construct an alternative future that would be in complete contrast to their present situation and a total contradiction of their past history. But in order to even begin to try to construct such an alternative future the people needed to discover the power to act against their conditioning. And they needed to do this while the personal, social, cultural, and political circumstances in which they were conditioned continued to be the dominant and dominating realities that circumscribed their lives. And that, they felt, was quite literally beyond them. Until, that is, one day God did something miraculous.

It was in the early years of our involvement with the Kanjars that it happened. The people were still quite nervous about making any innovations. But, more out of desperation than anything else, they had decided to go ahead with a primary health programme. They had built a hut for a clinic and a medical student had volunteered to help with basic health care.

For a while it seemed as if the programme might not only empower the community to deal with the diarrhoea problems, but that it might also help them with their despair. But at a critical stage in the development of this programme a child fell seriously ill. She was brought to the clinic for help but there was nothing that either the medical student or the other doctors she consulted could do to help. The diagnosis? Tetanus. The prognosis? Death.

We sensed that, if this child were to die, with her would die not only the hopes of her parents but also the hopes of all the other parents who had hoped against hope that, at long last, their lives might be different. So we did the only thing we could do at the time – we called the community together for prayer.

Everyone was, naturally enough, pretty sceptical about praying for the child. They had cried out to God to save their children many times in the past, but he never had. Their children died in their arms. But we told the Kanjars that we believed Jesus wanted to heal the child and that they should pray in the name of Jesus. We said we couldn't promise it would work, but it was our last best hope for this child.

So we all prayed in the name of Jesus for the child to live. I don't think any of us really believed that she would. We were just hoping against hope. Deep down we all expected her to die. But she didn't. Somehow, miraculously, she survived.

And that miracle made a significant difference in this community. It proved beyond doubt that things could be different. And that belief, that things could be different, unleashed the latent confidence in people that *they* could be different – in spite of their conditioning. And that confidence became the foundation of all the work that the Kanjars have done to develop the community since that day.

I remember talking to Ramu, a Kanjar leader, before I left India. I asked him what he thought were the most significant changes that had taken place in the Kanjar community. I shall never forget what he said. He said, 'Not everything is good. Many things are still bad. But it's a whole lot better than it was before. We have changed in many ways, Daud bhai. We believe God is for us. Not against us. We work things out better now in the community council. We do not have as many fights. These days us men spend less time taking drugs and getting stoned. We work in the garbage recycling co-op we have set up. We are able to bring in enough money – two or three times more than we used to get before – to meet more needs at home. Our wives are happier. Our children are healthier. And consequently not so many of our children die young anymore.'

I am not poor. I am rich. But I want to be with the poor in spirit. And as I identify with the poor in spirit I see that I am not the centre of the universe. The world does not revolve around me. My life is not all about me. My life is all about struggling with and for others who suffer. And, as I struggle with and for others who suffer, I find that over and over again I get to see a glimpse of heaven on earth.

2

We can be people who weep with those who weep, and we can see the difference it makes to the way we can relate to the world.

What we feel depends on what we see and hear, and what we see and hear depends on where we locate ourselves in the world. If we identify with the rich who are 'well fed' and 'laugh' (Luke 6:25), then we will 'laugh with those who laugh' (Rom. 12:15). But if we identify with the poor who 'go hungry' and 'weep' themselves to sleep (Luke 6:25), we will 'weep with those who weep' (Rom. 12:15)

• • •

Some time back I was asked by Tear Australia, a Christian aid and development agency I work for, if I would be willing to travel to the Sudan, the largest country in Africa, to assess the current situation there.

Needless to say I jumped at the chance to go. But, of course, I really didn't know what I was getting myself into.

This expedition that I made with Arthur McCutchan, from Kobokor in Northern Uganda to Kajo Keji in Southern Sudan, was one of the most hazardous excursions I have ever undertaken.

The road was pocked with bomb craters that were big enough to swallow trucks whole, and roving bands of armed robbers attacked vehicles that broke down on the road. As we were setting off we heard news that a convoy that had left barely an hour ahead of us had been shot to pieces by rebel soldiers.

But we had a job to do, so off we went. The drive to the border went without incident. It was dusk by the time we got to the outpost, and night fell fast and dark. There was no electricity. No light at all.

So at the checkpoint we were ordered to stop the car, turn off the headlights, and turn on the inside lights to illuminate the cabin of the car. We felt like sitting ducks – surrounded by soldiers with their fingers on their triggers, lit up like easy targets in a sideshow alley, and unable to see a thing.

What made us even more nervous was the fact that we were travelling on papers issued by the Sudan People's Liberation Army and, at the time we were asked to hand our documents out the window into the darkness, we weren't sure whether the soldiers that had us surrounded were government or guerrilla. The wrong ones – and we could have been in a bit of trouble. Fortunately, it was the SPLA at the border that night.

We crossed the border into Sudan. Sudan has a population of some thirty-five million people – Arab in the arid north, Negroid in the tropical south. They had been at war with one another for twenty-five of the last forty years.

It had been a particularly brutal war. Priests had been crucified. Captives were sold into slavery. Villages had been razed to the ground. And vital food stocks were destroyed. A million people had died. Five million people had been displaced, and ten million were at risk of starvation. Part of the problem was that government troops had been stopping emergency food supplies getting to the people in areas held by guerrillas.

At first sight, its gutted structures gave Kajo Keji the look of a ghost town. But it was inhabited by more than two hundred thousand people, many of them refugees seeking safety away from the fighting. But the bombed-out roads and bullet-ridden buildings indicated that even here the refugees were caught in the crossfire from time to time.

We met with a local pastor who greeted us warmly and offered to take us to visit some of the camps for displaced people around Kajo Keji. So we spent the day going around the town meeting groups of people squatting by the side of the road in temporary shelters made out of sticks and bits of blue plastic.

They told us their stories of fleeing on foot, from air raids and ground attacks, across hundreds of kilometres of inhospitable countryside. They all looked as if they'd walked as far as they could and couldn't walk another step to save themselves. A sign strung across the encampment read: 'Victory Is Assured'. But there was only defeat in the eyes of the bedraggled refugees.

The state of the emaciated people in the camps was serious. But it was more or less what I had expected. This kind of malnutrition is common in slums all over the world. But then I met the lepers.

The lepers were total outcasts, struggling to survive by scavenging on the outskirts of the camps. They didn't have access to a smidgen of the emergency supplies accessible to the people in the camps – not even a single aspirin between them in the last seven years. And nothing that I had ever experienced in India prepared me for the extremity of suffering I saw reflected in the lepers' eyes.

Minus their fingers and their toes, they dragged themselves around the edges of the camps in their skeletally thin bodies. Naked and broken, abandoned and alone, every move they made seemed to be like a silent scream, crying out:

'My God, my God, why have you forsaken me?' (Matt. 27:46)

That night we returned to base in Kajo Keji. I tried to sleep but couldn't. The sounds of screaming kept me awake.

At first I thought it might have been a domestic dispute. But as the screaming continued a chill crept up my spine. I realized that it was probably some poor man being tortured or some poor woman being raped. I got up to look around but I could see nothing in the impenetrable darkness.

I couldn't see anything. But I heard everything. I heard every howl of torment that was wrung from that wretched soul that night. It was excruciating for me to lie there listening to the screaming, but I knew it was hell for my unseen friend writhing at the hands of those merciless men.

At the time, the only thing I thought I could do was to pray. So I prayed, desperately, that the agony would end. But it went on and on. Like a wound that wouldn't heal.

I asked myself, 'Where is God now?'

And I heard a voice within me answer: 'Where is God now? He is here - writhing in agony at the hands of merciless men!'[1]

And I wept.

• • •

Time and time again I am reminded that I am called to live in sympathy with God and empathy with my neighbours. As I develop sympathy with God, I naturally develop empathy with my neighbours. And as I develop empathy with my neighbours who are in great pain, it inevitably entails great pain for me.

I have learned to 'wail' over the suffering in the world. I have learned to feel what I see and hear deep down in my soul and agonize over the suffering of others.

Jacques Attalli, the president of the European Bank for Reconstruction and Development, says that 'in the coming world order there will be winners and losers. (But) the losers will outnumber the winners by an unimaginable factor. They will yearn for the chance to live decently, and they are likely to be denied that chance.' Then, in a turn of phrase that is reminiscent of the fate of those consigned to the concentration camps I witnessed in the Sudan, he says, 'they will find themselves penned in, neglected by indifference'. And I tremble when he says: 'the horrors of the twentieth century will fade by comparison'.[2]

I have learned to 'lament' over the suffering in the world. I have learned to not only *feel* about what I see and hear but also to *think* about what I see and hear deep down in my soul and analyze the causes and the consequences of the suffering.

It's not enough for me to feel the pain. I need to think the pain through. 'Africa,' Attalli says, 'is a lost continent. It is one of the last places on earth in which famine persists.

The terrible facts of having fallen into an economic black hole speak for themselves: since 1970, Africa's share of the world's markets has been reduced by half; its debt has been multiplied by twenty and now equals its gross product; income in sub-Saharan Africa has fallen by a quarter since 1987. Falling exports and investments, coupled with aging machinery and equipment, guarantees that the economic plight will only grow worse.' And I can't stop thinking about Attalli's dire prediction that 'with the possible exception of South Africa, the most probable future of Africa is tragic: it will be totally lost'.[3]

I have learned to move from crying in silence to 'crying out loud' about the suffering in the world. I have learned to move beyond reflection about what I see and hear to action about what I see and hear. And I have come to understand the crying need to criticize our own personal and political complicity in the suffering of others.

Recently I went with a delegation to the office of Kevin Rudd, the Prime Minister of Australia who is my local Member of Parliament, and I had my say. When we entered the twenty-first century, these were the numbers (and they have not improved): of a population of over six billion people, almost five billion of these live in the 'developing' world. Four-fifths lack basic sanitation. One-third lack clean water. And one-fifth have no access to adequate health services.[4] Sure we give them aid. But we give them very little, and they are so indebted that for every dollar of aid we give to 'developing' countries, thirteen dollars come back in interest payments.[5] So, after decades of steady advance, aid and development have been thrown into reverse and over a billion hungry people are sliding, slowly but surely, into the abyss.[6] And even as we are going to press, the United States can find $700 billion to save Wall Street but the entire G8 can't find $25 billion dollars to save 25,000 children who die every day from preventable diseases!

I am not poor, but I want to be with the poor in spirit. And as I identify with the poor in spirit I see that my issues are not the centre of the universe. The world does not revolve around my concerns. Life – if it is all about love – should be all about loving others as myself. Loving others as myself involves feeling the pain of neighbours who are in pain. It involves weeping with those who weep. It involves wailing over their suffering. It involves lamenting over the causes and the consequences of their suffering. It involves crying out loud about our own personal and political complicity in the suffering of others.

3

**We can be people
who are meek,
angry yet restrained,**
and see the difference
it makes to the way
we can respond to
the world.

We ought to be angry about the injustice in the world. But we need to control our anger instead of being controlled by our anger. The question that we need to answer is this: How can we find a way to express our rage creatively with restraint?

• • •

This question was very much in my mind as I travelled through Pakistan to Afghanistan in search of the grave of Khan Abdul Ghaffar Khan.

As we were driving through the Khyber Pass I thought of the last time I had passed that way. It was in May 1973, and my wife and I were making a hasty retreat in the middle of a revolution. We were able to flee the jets that we saw flying menacingly over our heads, and the tanks that we had heard encircling the city of Kabul were far behind us. But, for the people of Afghanistan, there was no escape. They were about to face a quarter of a century of horrifying civil war.

It is impossible for any of us who were not there to comprehend the agony of that civil war. Statistics don't laugh. And statistics don't cry. But the figures do give us the bare bones of the tragedy that befell the people of Afghanistan.

The population of Afghanistan – between seventeen and eighteen million people – have seen the nightmare of one and a half million of their brothers and sisters being slaughtered before their very eyes. They have heard the moans of two and a half million of their neighbours lying wounded on the battlefield after the fighting was over. They have known the despair that comes with some six million of their countrymen and women fleeing in fear of their lives.

The once-proud capital of Kabul had been pounded into rubble. The traditional social infrastructure of Afghanistan had been almost completely destroyed. And the only industries that thrived – like gun running, drug dealing, and recycling the bones of dead comrades to sell as cooking oil – fed on the entrails of the broken body of the political economy like vultures.

On the way to Jalalabad, a city in eastern Afghanistan, I stared out of the window of my Land Rover at ravaged roads, ruined buildings, and arid plains littered with rocks and memories. Nothing moved except the slow shadow of a burnt-out tank rusting in the bright light of a pitiless sun and the fluttering flags on scrawny sticks, marking the otherwise unadorned and unattended graves of the *mujahadeen*.

There was more than a touch of irony about searching for the tomb of a man dedicated to non-violence in the middle of a war zone.

Upon arrival in Jalalabad we made our way through the back streets to the traditional fully-enclosed, high-walled, Afghan guest house where my brother and I had arranged to stay for a few days.

We were greeted by a very thoughtful manager who issued us with an extensive list of instructions which told us, among other things, that 'if there is fighting in the streets' we were to 'take refuge in the basement'. But 'if there is an earthquake' we were to flee the basement and 'take refuge in the streets'.

Needless to say, as we tried to get to sleep later that night, bedded down in the aforementioned basement, my brother and I found ourselves wide awake – pondering what we would do if we were hit by a seismic upheaval in the middle of a battle. But it had been a long journey and we were tired. So eventually worry gave way to weariness and we finally dropped off to sleep.

When we awoke, we decided to walk to the bazaar and talk to people about our search for the tomb of the Khan Abdul Ghaffar Khan. As is so often the case, what is a mystery to foreigners turned out to be a matter of common local knowledge. Every man and his dog knew where Khan Abdul Ghaffar Khan was buried in Jalalabad. Thus, with the crowd chorusing the vendor's blessing upon our pilgrimage, we were sent on our way – map in hand – to find the tomb of Badshah Khan in the backyard of a suburban house on the outskirts of Jalalabad.

When we arrived at the address we had been given we stood outside the house and banged on a battered wooden gate in the mud-brick wall that enclosed the compound. Someone eventually opened the door and the guardians of the tomb led us through the garden to see the grave of the late, great Khan Abdul Ghaffar Khan.

It's a simple grave made of gently-raised earth marked with rough-cut rocks, surrounded by the magnificent superstructure of a still as-yet-unfinished mausoleum.

When I first saw the crypt I felt an enormous sense of disappointment. While I felt the grave was appropriate for a man who had lived as simply and died as simply as he had, the mausoleum – the still as-yet-unfinished mausoleum – seemed all wrong to me.

However, as I talked with the guardians of the tomb about the amazing legacy of the Khan's life that, by and large, the world has failed to even notice, let alone honour, I began to realize that no memorial to Khan Abdul Ghaffar Khan could be more fitting than this still as-yet-unfinished mausoleum.

• • •

Abdul Ghaffar Khan was born in Utmanzai in 1890. His father, Behram Khan, was a wealthy Pathan who ran a large guest house on the main road to Peshawar. Behram Khan had many servants, but he always took great pride in serving his honoured guests himself. His mother – whose name I do not know – lived her life, like most Pathan women, in *purdah*, hidden from prying eyes behind a veil of secrecy. She was reputedly quite devout and set her son an unforgettable example of genuine piety.

In 1901 Ghaffar Khan attended Edwards Memorial School in Peshawar. The headmaster was Reverend Wigram, a stern but generous teacher who was committed to providing the best education he could for the boys on the North-West Frontier. The young Ghaffar Khan grew to appreciate him almost as much as he did his own parents. Not surprisingly then, after spending a couple of years in the Islamic school in Aligarh, in 1910 Ghaffar Khan started a school in his home town of Utmanzai.

In 1913 Ghaffar Khan participated in a conference of progressive Muslims that was held in Agra. He met famous Islamic leaders, like Maulana Azad, and he seized the opportunity to discuss his understanding of Islam with them. 'It is my inmost conviction,' he was to say later, 'that Islam is *amal* (work), *yakeen* (faith), and *muhabat* (love), and without these the name Muslim is sounding brass and tinkling cymbal.'[7]

Upon returning to the North-West Frontier after the conference, Ghaffar Khan decided to perform a *chilla*, or fast, in order to seek divine guidance regarding how he could put the *amal*, *yakeen*, and *muhabat* that he preached into practice. What actually occurred during the chilla no one knows. But we do know that Ghaffar Khan emerged from the fast with a resolute determination to serve God as fully as he could for the rest of his life.

He had married in 1912, and in 1915 his wife died of influenza. Ghaffar Khan then set out on a pilgrimage to visit every village in the North-West Frontier. Three years and five hundred villages later, Ghaffar Khan returned, saying; 'I have one great desire. I want to rescue these gentle people from the tyranny of the foreigners who have disgraced them. I want to kiss the ground where their ruined homes once stood. I want to wash the stains of blood from their garments. (And) I want to create for them a world of freedom, where they can live in peace, and be happy.'[8]

In 1919 Ghaffar Khan was arrested by the British authorities, who saw him as a threat to their power in the region. Over the next five years, Ghaffar Khan was in and out of prison for protesting against British imperialism. On one occasion he found himself grinding corn in solitary confinement. His fellow prisoners offered to pay a bribe to get him out of prison. But he refused. His prison guard told him he could stop grinding corn if he wanted to. But he replied, 'Robbers grind corn. And their cause is impure. Why should I mind grinding for my cause which is pure?'[9]

In 1924, after a three-year stretch in prison, Ghaffar Khan was released. He took the opportunity to go on a pilgrimage to Mecca. He was fascinated by the life of the Prophet, and especially by the early years when Mohammed spent his time in Mecca. Ghaffar Khan came back from his *haj* refreshed, armed with the 'weapon of the Prophet', and ready to re-engage in the struggle for freedom.

'The weapon of the Prophet', he says, 'is *sabr*', not 'a sabre'. The word literally means patience. 'The weapon of the Prophet', he says, 'is patience. If you exercise patience, endure all hardships, victory will be yours. No power on earth can stand against it.' He quotes the Koran as saying, 'there is no compulsion in religion'; 'forgive and be indulgent'; 'render not vain your almsgiving by injury'; 'whosoever killeth one – for other than manslaughter – it shall be as if he had killed all mankind, and whoso saveth the life of one, it shall be as if he had saved the life of all mankind'.[10]

In 1928 Ghaffar Khan started a newspaper called the *Pakhtun*. He would use this vehicle to rally his people for the long struggle. The following year Ghaffar Khan launched one of the most exciting, creative, and effective non-violent campaigns for independence ever conducted. It began innocuously enough, with the Khan calling Pathans to join him in forming a movement called the *Khudai Khidmatgar*. Any Pathan could join the movement, provided they swore an oath to become 'A Servant of God':

> I am a Khudai Khidmatgar, and as God needs no service . . .
>
> I promise to serve humanity in the name of God.
>
> I promise to refrain from violence, and from taking revenge.
>
> I promise to forgive those who oppress me or treat me with cruelty.
>
> I promise to refrain from taking part in feuds and quarrels.
>
> I promise to treat every Pathan as my neighbour and friend.
>
> I promise to live a simple life, to practice virtue, and refrain from evil.
>
> I promise to devote at least two hours a day to social work.[11]

For a Pathan, an oath such as this is a very serious matter. Once made, it cannot be broken – even upon pain of death. So in asking a Pathan to swear an oath such as this, Khan was hoping to appeal to the old warrior code to help forge a whole new warrior ethic. This ethic would pride itself on forgiveness rather than revenge, on service rather than slaughter, and would have the power to break the cycle of violence on the North-West Frontier once and for all.

It was a brilliant idea – culturally appropriate and politically astute. And Pathans responded to the Khan's call by rallying behind the banner of the *Khidmatgar* in their thousands. In fact, the recruiting drive was so successful that at one point up to one hundred thousand Pathans – men and women both – donned their famous red shirts and went to work in the villages, singing:

> We serve and we love; our people and our cause.
>
> Freedom is our longing; our lives the price we pay.[12]

The courage of these *Khudai Khidmatgar* was legendary. A British officer commanded a *Khidmatgar* by the name of Faiz Mohammed to take off his red shirt. He refused. The officer then commanded his soldiers to forcibly strip the recalcitrant. Faiz Mohammed did not fight back, but he refused to cooperate. It took up to nine soldiers to strip him of his proud red shirt. And even then they only were able to do it when they had beaten the *Khidmatgar* unconscious. The soldiers then came for a *Khidmatgar* by the name of Mohammed Naquib. He was beaten mercilessly and his shirt was stripped off his back. But when he was ordered to take off his trousers he went berserk. He turned to run to get a gun but was pulled up short by the voice of his commander. 'Mohammed Naquib!' he cried. 'Is your patience exhausted so soon?

You swore to remain non-violent until death!' With those words ringing in his ears, eyewitnesses say the chastened *Khidmatgar* turned back to face his tormentors, armed only with the 'weapon of the Prophet', fortitude, and forbearance.

A large crowd gathered in Kissa Khani Bazaar in Peshawar to protest the brutality of the British. Troops from a nearby army base were deployed. The troops asked the people to disperse and they had begun to do so when, without warning, three armoured cars drove at speed into the crowd. Several people were run over and killed on the spot. The troops again asked the people to disperse, but they said they would do so only if the armoured cars withdrew and they were allowed to carry away their fallen comrades. The troops did not remove their armoured cars and refused to allow the people to remove their fallen comrades. So the crowd did not disperse. The troops then opened fire, shooting point-blank range into the front row of the gathered throng. When those in the front row fell wounded, the next row came forward and took their places. Over and over again, from eleven o'clock in the morning till five o'clock in the evening, row upon row of *Khidmatgars* took the places of their fallen comrades, bared their breasts, and were shot to death by the troops. Between two and three hundred were killed, many more were wounded, and the bazaar was littered with piles of bodies of the dead and dying. The elite Garhwal Rifles were brought in to deal with the crowd. But, faced with unarmed men and women who would not fight, they refused to fire. 'We will not shoot our unarmed brethren!' they said. It was the beginning of the end for the empire on which, it was said, the sun would never set.[13]

In the aftermath of this protest Ghaffar Khan was arrested. He spent most of his time from 1930 to 1945 fighting for independence from prison. After independence Ghaffar Khan was finally released from prison, but then he was rearrested and thrown into prison once again – this time by the Pakistani government.

Ghaffar Khan had always supported Maulana Azad in his struggle for a liberal, secular, united, democratic country – and that had put him in conflict with Mohamed Ali Jinnah and the Muslim League's agenda for a Muslim State.

Khan said he feared a state founded on a religion – any religion – as he thought it would tend to discriminate against minorities. When Jinnah accused Khan of being less than earnest in his religion, he replied: 'I learned (my) secularism from the Koran Sharif.'[14] But it was not a view shared by the president of the 'Land of the Pure'. And, as a result, the redoubtable dissident was forced to spend most of the rest of his life – from 1948 to 1988 – either in jail in Pakistan or in exile in Afghanistan, where he finally died.

• • •

When I turned to an Afghan standing beside the tomb and asked him about his own reflections on the life of the Khan, he shrugged his shoulders. 'What can I say? He was failure. He fought for independence, and finished up in prison. He advocated non-violence, but ended up being buried in the middle of a civil war. Maybe he was a great leader, a *Badshah*, but nobody, not even Pathans, want to follow him.'

It was undoubtedly true. But was it the whole truth? Certainly he failed. But the Khan also succeeded where others before him, and after him, failed.

For one majestic moment in history the Khan had been able to turn some of the fiercest warriors in the world into some of the noblest soldiers the world has ever seen. They faced gun fire without flinching; they refrained from all forms of retaliation; they sought not to slaughter but to serve - friend and foe alike - in their fight for justice. I wondered how different Afghanistan might have been if the Pathans had followed the extraordinary example of their Badshah Khan Abdul Ghaffar Khan rather than the fundamentalist Taliban?

As I turned back to view the tomb once more before I left, the sun broke through the clouds and sent a shaft of light shining through the darkness, illuminating the saintly grave against the gloomy shadows that surrounded it. For me it was a sign - consider the life of the Khan!

How can we express our rage creatively and with restraint? Certainly as one of his followers I find the life of Jesus to be the supreme example. But because many Christians believe that Jesus was God incarnate, they think that his example of restraint is not relevant to ordinary mortals like you and me. I think the lives of ordinary mortals like Abdul Ghaffar Khan, Mahatma Gandhi, and the Dalai Lama prove that the example of Jesus *is* relevant to all people of all religions.

The core of the challenge for me, in expressing my rage creatively, is to practice the patience, the *sabr*, that is, as the Khan said, at the heart of restraint.

I need to be patient with myself. I need to remember that my rage is a powerful force that can motivate me to act in spite of the forces arrayed against me. But I also need to remember that if I don't control my rage it will control me – and it could cause me to act in a destructive way against those who oppose me.

The first step for me in controlling my rage is to *acknowledge* my rage. I have come to realize that I cannot control my rage by suppressing or repressing my feelings, or by pretending that my feelings are other than they are. But I can manage my rage by being aware of and attentive to my feelings, and by dealing with my feelings, for better or worse, as they really are.

The second step for me in controlling my rage is to *ventilate* my rage against my 'enemies' in prayer. This is a great biblical tradition practised by the psalmists. But, according to the Bible, prayer is the only place I should ever ventilate uncensored rage – because God is the *only* one who can take my destructive anger and transform it into a constructive force.

The third step for me in controlling my rage is to *transform* my rage by beginning to pray *for* my 'enemies' rather than *against* them. After all, Jesus said the best way for us to exorcise our desire for revenge is to 'turn the other cheek' (Matt. 5:39), and the best way for us to extend grace in the face of injustice is to 'bless those who curse you, pray for those who mistreat you' (Luke 6:28).

It is then – and only then – that I can practice patience with my opponents.

It is only then that I can be truly mindful of the fact that while my 'enemies' are people I don't like and/or who don't like me, they are still people just like me and need to be treated with the respect I cherish – in spite of our grievances.

I don't know whether I could ever practice *sabr* to the extent that the *Khudai Khidmatgar* did in Kissa Khani Bazaar, but I pray that if I was called to do so, I would.

> *I am not poor, but I want to be with the poor in spirit. As I identify with the poor in spirit, I see the need to stand in solidarity with those who suffer. In order to stand in solidarity with those who suffer, I need to confront those who cause their suffering. I need to be angry enough to act, but not so angry that I act aggressively. I need to practice patience with myself and with my opponents – acknowledging my rage, ventilating my rage, and transforming my rage into a respectful engagement.*

4

**We can be people
who seek to
do right by others**
and see the difference
it makes to the way
that we can engage
our world.

When Jesus blessed those 'who hunger and thirst for righteousness', he wasn't commending people who were obsessed with their 'self-righteousness'. Rather, he was commending people who passionately seek 'to do right by others'.

• • •

For more than ten years, Ange and I and our two children lived in the cosmopolitan city of Delhi.

The imperial splendour of Rajpath is superb. The quiet beauty of Lodhi Gardens is enchanting. And the hustle and bustle on Chandni Chowk is exciting. But it is the people – the millions of people who crowd into the city from all over India – who make Delhi such a colourful place to live. It is the meeting of Kashmiris, Punjabis, and Rajasthanis; the Nagas, Mizos, and Manipuris; the Biharis, Bengalis, and Oriya; and the Telegus, Tamils, and Malayalis that made the poet Ghalib once describe Delhi as 'the soul in the body of the world'.

We lived in an intentional poly-ethnic residential community called Aashiana, which included twenty-one non-Indians and thirty-three Indians. Of the non-Indians, thirteen of us were from Australia, four from England, three from Canada, and one from Germany. Of the Indians, sixteen were from Delhi itself, six from Punjab, five from Goa, three from Maharashtra, two from Tamil Nadu, and one from Andhra Pradesh. Almost half of the marriages were international and almost all of the marriages, including our own, were cross-cultural.

Not only was the group international and cross-cultural, it was also multi-faith. The majority of us were Christian, but there were also quite a few Hindus, a Muslim, a Buddhist, and a Jain. At different times, we all lived in the same six-bedroom house. Believe it or not, from time to time up to fifty people stayed in the house at the same time – and, believe it or not, we all absolutely loved it.

As a community, we were enchanted by a vision of heaven on earth – intoxicated with passion for God and compassion for our neighbours. The Sermon on the Mount became our manifesto. We welcomed strangers. We shared meals with guests round our table. We ate joy and sorrow. We drank to redemption. We cared for the sick, addicted, and abused. And gladly we shared our wealth with the poor. As a community we were committed to working for justice with marginalized groups of people in the city of Delhi.

Our praxis was akin to Gandhiji's. Aashiana, like Gandhi, called people to a commitment to '*sarvodaya*', or service to all, starting with the 'last' 'first' and doing the 'most' with the 'least'. We turned our home into a rehab community for young people addicted to heroin and other drugs – helping them on the condition that they would help others. It wasn't long before we had a large team of the recovering addicts from *Sahara* (which is what we called our rehab work) helping us in *Sharan* (which is what we called our development work), doing voluntary work with the poorest of the poor in the slums around the city of Delhi.

Ange and I think back on that time as a biblical dream come true, and we have never forgotten it. A saying etched in a wall in Lal Quila, Shah Jahan's Red Fort in Delhi, expressed our feelings perfectly. 'If on earth there is a place of bliss, it is this, it is this, it is this.'[15]

Then one day all hell broke loose. The prime minister Indira Gandhi was assassinated by her Sikh bodyguards. People went crazy and took to the streets. Wherever they could find Sikhs they grabbed them by their long, uncut hair, held them down, poured petrol over them and set them alight. Mobs stopped buses and stormed trains, searching for Sikhs. They pulled people off at random, cutting them to pieces as they struggled to escape.

In most places the police were completely unprepared. Where they were prepared they were totally outnumbered. One police inspector in Vasant Vihar confronted a mob single-handedly. However, incidents of such courage were exceptional. The police were unable – or unwilling – to do much about it. The mobs ruled the streets.

Wherever they went, these mobs of weapon-wielding maniacs – driven mad by grief and anger and years of terrible suppressed frustration – looted and burned everything they could lay their hands on. Soon billowing columns of smoke rose from vehicles, petrol stations, department stores, factories and houses that were all ablaze. People clambered to their roofs to witness the sight of buildings all over the city in flames, burning like thousands of funeral pyres. In less than twenty-four hours, more than three thousand Sikhs – who up until that time had been living peacefully with their neighbours for decades – were slaughtered senselessly on the streets of Delhi.

I knew that I had to do something. But '*kya kare yaar?*' – 'what to do?' Up until then we had practiced Gandhi's '*savodaya*', or 'constructive action', but we had never really practiced Gandhi's '*satyagraha*', or 'non-violent intervention'.

I felt totally inadequate and terribly afraid. It's one thing to talk about the risks we need to take when we don't need to take any; it's another thing to actually take the risks we talk about when we need to take them. I knew that this was my moment of truth. Yet, at that moment, I was tempted to do anything but take the risk I knew I had to take to make a stand.

To my shame, I must admit, I was so frightened that doing nothing seemed infinitely preferable to doing something that might be very scary. However, I knew in my spirit that if I didn't do something to stand by my Sikh neighbours against the Hindu backlash it would be a complete contradiction of everything I had ever said about my dream of neighbours standing by their neighbours in their hour of need.

I discussed it with Ange and we decided we had to do something – although we didn't know what. We talked it over with our friends in the community.

Luke and Meera decided to stay on in their house to support the Sikh families living upstairs and downstairs in their building. Aashwini, Hoshang, and Sundar went to stay with a Hindu neighbour who wanted help protecting two Sikhs who were staying with him – one of whom had been badly beaten by a mob on a rampage, had barely escaped with his life, and was feeling petrified. The rest of us in Aashiana decided to make our households available as sanctuaries for Sikhs seeking refuge.

As the word spread, Sikhs fled to us. We closed the windows, drew the curtains, locked the doors, and prayed that the mobs would pass us by. Ange remembered an elderly Sikh builder staying on a building site across the road from our house and sent me to get him. I crept across the road, snuck him into our house, and hid him in our bedroom.

This was all good, but it wasn't really good enough. It was essentially a passive, rather than an active, approach to intervention. I couldn't imagine that the Khan, or the Mahatma, or Christ himself would have settled for such a passive approach when there was such a desperate need for active non-violent intervention. But I couldn't imagine doing what they did. What was I to do? That was the question I had to answer.

Ange and I talked it over further. She said that whatever I decided to do needed to be guided by the Spirit – and not driven by some deep-seated un-dealt-with messianic complex. However, she also said she knew in her spirit that if her father, brother, or son were in danger she would want someone like me to try to save them.

My friend Tony had a similar desire to do something more, so we decided to go out on my motorbike to see if we could find Sikhs under siege. I think I had the brilliant idea that we'd drive around until we saw a mob chasing a Sikh, then we'd race in alongside them and get ahead of them so that Tony could grab their intended victim and put him on the back of the bike. Then I'd turn on the power and we'd zoom off into the sunset. But, not surprisingly, it didn't actually work out like that.

We had just set off on our mission when we turned a corner not far from our house and ran straight into a mob of over a hundred people wielding knives, swords, and an assortment of wooden clubs and iron bars. We stopped, got off the bike, took a few deep breaths to calm our nerves, and walked over to talk to the mob.

'*Namaste. Kya hal hai?* What are you guys doing here?' I asked them.

'We're here to kill some Sikhs!' they answered straightaway, smiling. 'What are you doing here?' they asked me in return.

'I'd rather not say,' I replied rather reluctantly.

'Tell us,' they insisted.

'You wouldn't believe it, even if I told you,' I said.

'Try us!' they cried.

'Well, believe it or not,' I said. 'We're here to stop you from killing anybody.'

They laughed. I laughed, too. It was rather ridiculous to think that there was anything a couple of unarmed men could do to prevent an armed mob going on a rampage.

'Let's see what happens,' they said. 'We're going to wait here for a bus, check out the passengers, and once we get our hands on one of those bastards we're going to cut him to pieces. It'll be fun to see what you're going to do about that!'

While they waited for a bus, we waited with them. I used the time to chat with them about their families and talk to them about my own wife and children. I was hoping that when the moment of confrontation came they would relate to me as a nice man with a wife and two children, rather than as a disposable stranger.

A bus came along. They jumped aboard and searched high and low. No Sikhs. They got off, disgruntled. Another bus came along. They jumped aboard and searched high and low. Still no Sikhs. As they got off, their anger turned to rage. They marched off to a shopping centre where they smashed their way into the shops and set them on fire. But they quickly abandoned the shopping centre and marched up the road towards an estate. It was blood, not loot, they wanted.

We jumped on the motorbike again and raced ahead of the mob to try to organize some neighbourhood resistance to the invasion.

'They are going to kill the Sikhs!' I cried.

'Serves them right!' the Hindus in the neighbourhood association replied.

We were wondering what to do next when a cry rang out that grabbed us by the scruff of our necks. The rabble had come across a post box with the name 'Singh' printed on it, suggesting Sikhs in residence. They'd broken into the house and the family had fled to the patio on the roof, where they were calling for help.

We raced to the spot, pushed our way through the crowd, and took our stand between the mob and the family, at the bottom of the stairs. We faced the horde with our hands held together in a gesture of peace, and we pleaded for peace.

'*Shanti. Shanti.* Peace. Peace. *Unko na marna.* Don't hurt them,' we prayed.

The mob broke down the door, busted up the furniture, and threatened to butcher us if we didn't let them through. We were tempted to run, but we stood our ground at the bottom of the stairs. They took the petrol cap off my motorbike, threw a match into the petrol tank to set it on fire, and threatened to do the same to us if we didn't let them through.

Our hearts were pounding, our palms were sweating, and our knees were literally shaking – but we stayed where we were. For a moment our fate hung in the balance. If one of them hit us, we knew that all of them would follow suit – cutting us to pieces or setting us on fire like all the other mobs did that day.

But they hesitated. And, as they hesitated, the moment of danger disappeared as quickly as it had come. They broke ranks, spat curses at us, turned their backs on us, and walked away.

When it was safe, we called out to the family who were still huddled on the roof. They came down the stairs very warily, looking around to make sure the mob had gone. When they saw it was all clear we greeted each other, hugged one another, then sat down on the front steps and wept together with relief.

A little while later the army arrived in armoured cars and deployed squadrons of soldiers all over the troubled area, with orders to shoot to kill rioters on sight.

The rabble fled. And we were left to work out how we were going to get home.

. . .

In crises such as these, the Spirit always prompts us to be who, deep down, we really want to be – and to do what we deeply, truly, madly want to do. If you are like me, you will probably be tempted to think there is nothing you can do. But, in retrospect, I think there is always something we can do if we listen to the still, small voice of the Spirit. The little we can do may not make a lot of difference – but it may make the difference between life and death!

Each of us who feels inadequate needs to realize our capacity to act. And each of us who feels afraid needs to realize our courage to act. Each of us who feels impotent needs to recognize the potential of our actions. And each of us who feels insignificant needs to recognize the consequences of our actions.

Every act of truth is a victory over lies. Every act of love is a victory over hatred. Every act of justice is a victory over brutality. Every act of peace is a victory over bloodshed. And every risk a person takes to make a stand, no matter how small it may be, is a victory in the battle for a better world.

I am not poor, but I want to be with the poor in spirit. As I identify with the poor in spirit, I see the need to stand in solidarity with those who suffer. In order to stand in solidarity with those who suffer, I need to confront those who cause their suffering. I need to be angry enough to act, but not so angry that I act aggressively. I need to practice patience with myself and with my opponents. I need to acknowledge, ventilate, and transform my rage into a respectful engagement. In that engagement I should not attack others but should protect others from attack. Though I am fearful, I need to listen to the still, small voice saying 'be not afraid'. Being committed to a spirit of peace, in danger I need to put my body on the line.

5

We can be people who treat others as we ourselves would like to be treated and see the difference it makes to the way that we can initiate real change.

Jesus blesses those who seek justice but reminds us that true justice always needs to be full of mercy. As far as Jesus is concerned, it is impossible for any of us to do justice to one another unless we show the same mercy to others as we would hope – and pray – for others to extend to us in our need.

• • •

Some time back, the landlords in our neighbourhood went into a rent hike frenzy. The vulnerable people in our locality who depended on cheap rental accommodation were freaking out.

A number of community meetings were called to come up with a plan to solve the problem. One suggestion was guerrilla warfare led by chainsaw-wielding storm troopers who would cut the power brokers off at the knees! The idea received a spontaneous avalanche of applause. But after the applause died down, everyone acknowledged that the prospect was repugnant.

I sat in the meeting trying to think of an approach that would free us to confront the issues effectively but in a manner that was respectful of everyone, including our opponents. Eventually an idea came to me and I got to my feet and strode to the front of the room.

'I feel I need to go on a hunger strike. To fight against the greed that's wrecking our community. And to fight for the rights of everyone in our community, whether they are rich or poor, to have affordable access to secure tenancy.'

People clapped. So I continued to speak.

'I'm not going to break my fast until fifty landlords promise not to increase their rents by more than ten per cent; until fifty tenants promise to support responsible landlords and expose irresponsible landlords; until fifty residents promise to help landlords and tenants negotiate a just settlement of this dispute by publicly commending those who do and publicly condemning those who don't!'

People cheered. So the plan was carried.

After the meeting a young man called Steve Haynes came and spoke to us about the plan. Steve said he liked the plan because it was active, because it addressed the issues for all the parties in the dispute, and because it called upon the factions in our community to fight together non-violently for a common cause. We said we would be glad if Steve could join us in putting the plan into action. So Steve signed on for the campaign.

Each day a few people would join me on my hunger strike in Boundary Street – collecting signatures of landlords, tenants, and residents who promised to help us to solve the rental problem in West End.

One landlord agreed not to raise his rents at all. Another landlord, responding to an appeal by his tenants over the matter of a raise in rent imposed by a real estate agent, fired the real estate agent and fixed the rent back at the original rate. Yet another owner, upon discovering that his tenants were going through a tough time financially, actually reduced the rent for a period of time.

All of these landlords were presented with bunches of flowers to commend them for their sense of responsibility. The presentations took place on national television to encourage them, and others like them, to continue to act as responsible citizens in our community.

Steve was amazed that we had been able to get so many landlords on our side, and he was amused by our tactics for keeping them there. We talked with Steve about the line dividing good and evil not running between classes, such as landlords and tenants, but right down the middle of every individual – landlords, tenants, the residents, the lot. And we talked with Steve about the potential that all of us, landlords as well as tenants, have to respond to the challenge to renounce evil and embrace good.

However, not everybody responded well to the challenge of renouncing the evil of capitalism and embracing the good of the community. One landlord in particular proved to be totally ruthless in his pursuit of a profit. He beat up his tenant, a woman by the name of Kimberly Williams, who could not pay the inordinate rent he demanded. Then he literally threw her down the stairs in his haste to get her out of his flat as quickly as he could. Ange and I went to talk with Kimberly. We listened to the story and were convinced of its veracity. We assured her of our support. And we became firm friends.

Ange and I then went to talk with the landlord. The landlord was Greek, as is Ange. We hoped the Greek-Australian connection would make our communication easier. But the landlord was not interested in anything we had to say – even when we spoke in Greek. He told us he had the right to run his business in any way he wanted. We tried to suggest that he had the right to run his business any way he wanted as long as he didn't infringe on the rights of others to safety and security. He told us we had no right to call him to account since he was only accountable to himself, his family, and his bank balance. When we challenged that, he told us to get out and threatened to kill us if we ever came back. As far as he was concerned, we were mortal enemies.

Because we were afraid, we felt like backing off. But we also felt constrained to be faithful to the cause in spite of the death threat hanging over our heads. So we organized a group of residents to camp out on this landlord's doorstep, to bring home to him the reality of the homelessness that his callousness was causing.

In order to conduct the protest respectfully, we asked everyone involved to make sure they didn't block any entrances, didn't break any property, and always spoke to the landlord politely – in spite of provocation to do otherwise. While we were camped on his doorstep we discussed the issues with the landlord, his family, and with his neighbours. But while some of his neighbours were very supportive and some of his family were very sympathetic, the landlord himself was totally unwilling to negotiate.

The landlord kept a big pot simmering on the stove all night and told us he was just itching for us to give him an excuse to pour boiling water over us. And he might well have done so had the police not kindly agreed to drive by regularly to make sure he didn't lose his cool and scald us all.

Because this man was so aggressive and so prone to violence and threats of violence, we feared that he might take out his frustration on his family. So we organized a team of people he knew (though he didn't know they were associated with us) to drop in to check on his family.

In spite of all our efforts, the landlord steadfastly refused to apologize to Kimberly or reinstate her as a tenant. So we eventually were forced to take him to court to hold him accountable for his vicious assault. When he was found guilty we requested that the judge sentence him with six months of community work with us – in the hope that we could sort things out by serving the community together. He never did figure us out, though, and he was furious with us till the day he died.

But nine days into the fast we had the backing of fifty landlords who promised not to increase their rents by more than ten per cent, fifty tenants who agreed to support responsible landlords and expose irresponsible landlords, and fifty residents who had offered to help landlords and tenants negotiate just settlements. These people not only did a tremendous amount themselves, but they also put a lot of pressure on various levels of government to do even more. Because of this we were able to organize a series of community consultations that grew into the most comprehensive process in town planning in which the Brisbane City Council had ever engaged. And, as a result, affordable housing was put back on the agenda for our area.

So, on the tenth day, we broke our fast with doner kebabs at a local Lebanese restaurant.

Kimberly, the tenant on whose behalf we had fought, came to believe in us through the part we had played in supporting her through the conflict. In fact, Jim and Anne from the local Catholic Worker community took Kimberly into their home. She stayed with them on and off for years until she got a housing commission flat of her own. During the time she stayed with them, Jim and Anne shared with Kimberly the faith in Christ that sustains their 'amazing' lifestyle. And though she says she'll never share their 'crazy' lifestyle, Kimberly has come to share Jim and Anne's faith in Christ.

Steve, the young man who had joined our campaign at the beginning, was intrigued by how constructively we had managed the conflict. We had checked out the facts. We had chatted face-to-face with the landlord and the tenant. We had confronted the landlord clearly and cogently and called him to account for his actions. We had cared for the tenant simply and practically by helping her with alternative accommodation. And we had seen the conflict through to a resolution – in spite of the death threats – being as respectful as we possibly could be in the process.

'That's a great way to go,' Steve told us. 'It's a really creative way to approach conflict resolutions. Where did you guys get the idea from?'

'You may find it hard to believe,' we told him. 'But the way we've been trying to deal with things round here is the way Christ taught people to do it!'

'That's incredible!' Steve said. 'Most of the Christians I know aren't even interested in housing issues, let alone in dealing with housing disputes through direct action.'

We found out that Steve had been brought up as a Catholic and had gone to Mass regularly with his mum. At one time he'd been quite devout, but he'd decided to chuck it all in, he said, because they were 'so conservative' and 'had no answers to the bigger questions' he'd been asking about global justice.

'Well,' we said, 'if you read the Gospels you'll find that Christ was not only very committed to the poor, and the issues that had an impact on the poor, but he was also prepared to take action, even direct action, to stand with the poor against those who oppressed them.'

So Steve went off with renewed resolve to scrap everything he'd learned, or thought he'd learned, about Christianity thus far and to get properly acquainted with the Christ that strode through the pages of the Gospels. A little later we met up with Steve again. He told us that he'd read the Gospels and was so impressed with the person he'd encountered in the Scriptures that he'd begun to look to Christ as a guide for making some major decisions about the way he wanted to live his life.

Steve began to get together with a bloke by the name of Peter Westoby – who was a member of the Waiters' Union at the time – and with Peter's support he began to make some big changes in his life. Eventually, Steve decided to cultivate a sustainable rhythm of work and rest which maximized his creativity and minimized his stress and helped him manage his own mental and emotional health a whole lot better. Then he got involved with helping to organize Grow, a peer counselling group that worked to empower people with a range of physical and psychiatric disabilities to make the most of their lives.

At the same time as all this was happening, Steve was getting to know the local Catholic Workers. For Steve, getting to know Jim and Anne was like coming home. They were Catholic, but – unlike any other Catholics Steve had met – they were anarchists just like him. The Catholic Workers, with their radical response to global issues, were just the kind of people Steve had been looking for all his life. With Jim and Anne's encouragement, Steve and his partner Judy slowly but surely managed to develop a way of life that has become the envy of all the anarchists I know. With their two children Julia and Christopher, Steve and Judy live in secure tenant-managed accommodation which is owned by their housing co-operative. Steve has developed his own self-managed employment programme, a carpentry business, building beautiful furniture and restoring old houses. His business is working so well it's still thriving – even in the recession.

Steve and Judy also play a vital part in sustaining the ethos of the Waiters' Union. They not only take their own initiatives but also support the initiatives that other people in the network take towards community development in the neighbourhood. Steve has been involved in helping with a Boarding House Project that provides affordable housing for people who are disadvantaged. And Judy has been involved in helping at the Bristol Street Household providing hospitality, company, and emergency accommodation for people in distress.

There are no quick fixes. It's only when we treat others as we'd like to be treated ourselves that we can build a better world – bit by bit – out of the ruins of our broken dreams.

If I am to treat others as I hope they would treat me, I need to always be mindful of treating people with respect – in spite of any real or perceived grievances that we may have against one another. I need to be mindful of the impact that the struggle over the grievance may have on the most vulnerable people in my community. I need to be mindful of the significant needs of each party to the dispute – and especially the needs of my opponents. I need to be mindful of the significant fears of each party to the dispute, including the fears I have of my opponents and the fear they may have of me. I need to be mindful of looking for common ground with others – including my opponents. And I need to keep on looking until I find at least one thing that I have in common with them – and, once I have found it, I need to hold it close to my heart. I need to treat any common ground I have with people as holy ground and take off my big boots, walk in my bare feet, and tread as lightly as I can around tender areas.

6

We can be people who act with integrity and see the difference that it makes to the way that we can activate true change.

Jesus expects us to be 'perfect' as our heavenly Father is 'perfect' (Matt. 5:48). What Jesus is expecting in terms of 'perfection' is that we 'realize our potential'. We are created in the image of God to reflect the love of God in our lives as faithfully as we can. So, as far as Jesus is concerned, for us to be 'perfect' we need to let the light of the love of God so shine in our lives that people will see our 'good deeds' and 'glorify our Father in heaven' (Matt. 5:16).

• • •

It was our parents who taught me and my wife Ange to act with integrity. They showed us that it was possible for people – ordinary people like you and me – to practice the transformative initiatives of Jesus and, in so doing, to realize our potential to reflect the love of God practically in our everyday lives.

Our parents helped us learn to live according to the guidelines that Jesus gave his disciples in the Sermon on the Mount. Through them we learned to pray authentically in secret and to make the Lord's Prayer the prayer of our heart. They taught us to seek the kingdom of heaven on earth and not to worry about riches or status but to care for the poor, to give aid when asked, to turn the other cheek when attacked, to take the log out of our own eye before trying to extract the speck from another's.

My mother and father, Frank and Margaret Andrews, wanted above all else to reflect the love of God practically in their lives. My parents showed God's love in their love for one another. I have many memories of seeing my parents cuddling in the kitchen and hearing them talk endearingly to one another at the dinner table. My parents also showed God's love in their love for their kids. One of my most significant memories of my father is of him hugging me and telling me how much he loved me, over and over and over again. My father made it easy for me to believe in the love of God. I saw it, heard it, and felt it every day of my life.

But my parents didn't just show God's love in their love for their own family. They also expressed God's love in their love for human family in general. They regularly took people they had never met before into their hearts. Our home was always open to strangers in distress. People going through difficult times would stay for a day, a year, or however long they needed. As a young impressionable boy I can remember the excitement that some of those people brought to our house. A cat burglar who had just been released from jail showed us how easy it was to break into our house. And my parents never bothered locking the house after that!

My parents always tried to do 'the right thing'. If they didn't, they were quick to acknowledge it and apologize for it. I can remember one occasion when my father had chastised me for some misdemeanour but, upon reflection, he felt he had been unfair to me. So before he went to bed he came into my bedroom, knelt down by my bed and asked me if I would forgive him. Here was the highest authority figure I knew, on his knees, seeking to make things right with me.

Ange's parents, James and Athena Bellas, operated the Star Milk Bar in downtown Brisbane. It was famous for its food and drink and people would come from all over town for a fresh salad sandwich and a mango milkshake. Every morning, very early, my father-in-law would open up the café. When he did, it seemed like all the hobos round town would emerge from the hiding places where they had huddled for the night and make their way to the cafe. My father-in-law would welcome them in, sit them down, serve them tea and toast, and chat with them about the night they'd had and the day ahead.

If anyone needed a job my father-in-law would leave his brothers in charge of the café and go job-hunting with them. If they got in trouble with the police, he would visit them in prison. He regularly visited those who got sick and wound up in hospital. When anyone friendless died, my father-in-law would make sure that he went to their funeral – so that no one would be buried without a friend. Often he'd be the only one there.

Ange's dad would also invite folk home to share a meal with the family – even though they already had eight children of their own to feed. If anything, meals at the Bellas' house were even more famous than the milkshakes at the Star Milk Bar, so there was never a shortage of people who were willing to take up the invite – or just invite themselves.

Ange's large family was always being enlarged to make room for one more, and in this way her parents taught her the importance of being family to those who had no family.

The Greek practice of *symbetheri* is profound reciprocal regard for family – but Ange's family totally revolutionized the traditional practice of *symbetheri* when they included people whom Greeks traditionally excluded – their enemies, the Turks! Frank and Margaret Andrews and James and Athena Bellas have been shining examples as they have demonstrated how we can 'let our light so shine' that people will see the love of God reflected in our lives.

• • •

Jesus says that it is only when we are 'pure' of heart ourselves that we will see God – and God's love – truly reflected in our lives (Matt. 5:8). One of the issues I have struggled with personally is how we can try to be pure without being 'puritanical' and/or becoming a 'purist'.

My friend CB Samuel, who is a well-known Indian Christian leader and all-round good guy himself, often tells the story of how a goldsmith in his country removes the imperfections in his gold. CB explains that the goldsmith heats the gold over a fire until it melts. Then he looks for all the impurities that float to the surface of the molten gold and picks them out, one by one, till none are left. The goldsmith, CB says, can tell the gold is pure when he can see his face perfectly reflected in its surface.

I think that is a brilliant analogy of what God wants to do in our lives. God wants to melt our hearts in the fire of struggling with the suffering in the world so that all the impurities in our lives can float to the surface. Over the course of our times of struggle God helps us to pick out these impurities, one by one. Each time this happens we become more truly and purely compassionate and are better able to see the love of God reflected in our lives until, one day, no impurities will be left.

I have found that any efforts I make to deal with the 'impurities' in myself by introspection only make me more selfish, not less selfish. This is because I become preoccupied with my own improvement as a person – and that is essentially a selfish process. It tends to make me 'self-righteous' rather than 'righteous' – which is completely counterproductive.

I remember with some embarrassment one of my earliest attempts to deal with my own selfishness. As usual, given my flair for melodrama, my effort to deal with my selfishness was a flawed heroic affair. I was sick and tired of being selfish, so I decided that I would stay inside my house and set aside a whole month to fast and pray until I was sure that I could emerge from my suburban cell – like a butterfly from a cocoon – brilliantly and beautifully selfless.

I actually followed through on my resolution and hungrily paced around the empty rooms of my house for four long weeks, praying that every thought and feeling I had would be selfless. But the catch was this: the more I prayed about trying to be less self-conscious, the more self-conscious I became about trying to be less self-conscious. So I emerged at the end of the month more self-centred than when I had started!

Since that time I have discovered that the best way to deal with my selfishness is not by trying to conquer myself in an epic struggle, but by simply trying to become more conscious of others in the midst of my daily life.

It seems to me that Jesus dealt with any temptation to selfishness not by turning to introspection, but by giving up any preoccupation he might have had with himself and giving himself, wholeheartedly, to the service of God. Jesus demonstrated how he allowed his Father to set the agenda for his life when he said to his friends, 'I don't do anything on my own account. I only do what I see the Father doing' (John 5:19). As far as Jesus was concerned, 'doing the Father's will' was where it was at for him. He explained, 'I have food and drink that you don't know anything about. My food and my drink is to do the Father's will' (John 4:32, 34).

For Jesus, 'doing the Father's will' meant living a life of service to others. 'I have come not to be served, but to serve, and to give my life as the sacrifice I want to make in serving others' (Matt. 20:28). And it was in that furnace of service for others that Jesus was forced to deal with the issues that arose for him.

I have learned that I need to do the same. I need to simply commit myself to love God and to love my neighbour as myself – and to deal with the issues about myself that I need to address in order to love well as and when they arise. Most of the issues which arise for me are no surprise to me or to those who know me. The reality is that all of us struggle with the 'seven deadly sins' to some degree or other. And I need to deal with my lust, my gluttony, my greed, my sloth, my wrath, my envy, and my pride like everybody else.

One of the issues that arose for me during the landlord-tenant-resident campaign which did take me by surprise was how easily tempted I was to use the campaign to enhance my own profile. It seemed innocent enough until I realized that using a campaign to enhance my own profile involved using other people's pain to promote myself – and that was equivalent to exploiting a situation of exploitation for my own ends. To deal with my temptation to do this I adopted Jesus' guideline of 'not letting my left hand know what my right hand was doing' (Matt. 6:8). For me, this meant making a commitment that, after the campaign was over, I would not take on any high-profile, public protests for a year but would rather give myself to low-profile, anonymous acts of service round the area.

I believe that, in order to be the change I want to see in the world, I need to act with integrity. Otherwise I will inevitably become the very problem that I am trying to solve. To act with integrity, I need to deal with my own contradictions. But in order to deal with my own contradictions in a healthy way, I believe I need to simply commit myself to love God and to love my neighbour as myself – and to deal with the issues I need to address in order to love well as they arise. Like many others, I have a proverb playing in a loop in my head that says: 'if it's worth doing, it's worth doing well; if it's worth doing, it's worth doing well; if it's worth doing, it's worth doing well'. And because I'm often unsure of my capacity to do things well right from the start, I'm often scared to start. But I've come to believe that anything that is good enough to do is worth doing badly to begin with. But if I really want to do good, then each time I have a go at something I should do better. And there are no better guidelines for me as to how I can do better than to practice the transformative initiatives of Jesus, as my parents did before me.

7

We can be people who work for peace and see the difference that it makes to the way that we can actuate non-violent change.

Jesus explicitly, specifically, and repeatedly contradicted the Mosaic law that legitimated retaliation. 'You have heard that it was said, "Eye for eye, and tooth for tooth." But I tell you, Do not resist [or retaliate against] an evil person. If someone strikes you on the right cheek, turn to him the other also' (Matt. 5:38–39). Jesus told his disciples, 'you should always be ready to die – but never to kill – for your faith' (Matt. 16:24). So the Jesus movement should be a peace movement.

• • •

My father wasn't a Christian during World War II. But my mother was. And, as a Christian, she was a committed pacifist. Because she was a pacifist, she was called a coward. To prove she wasn't a coward, my mother used to run messages from one air raid shelter to another during the air raid bombings.

Not surprisingly, my mother brought me up to be a pacifist – the kind of pacifist who does not use pacifism as an excuse for cowardice, but who rather understands pacifism as a framework for courageous intervention in the context of violence. I've intervened in many violent situations in my life. Sometimes I've been beaten up so badly I've had to be hospitalized. One time I had to be rushed in for emergency surgery. But that was when I was younger and intervened more aggressively, unconsciously escalating the spiral of violence in the situation. Now that I'm older, I'm a little wiser. These days I am very wary about intervening and, when I do, I am very careful to do so as peacefully as possible. My fear doesn't usually stop me. But it does usually slow me down – which is exactly what fear ought to do. It shouldn't stop us, but it should slow us down and make us more careful about how we go about the task of getting involved with people.

One night I was walking down the street and came across a man being attacked by a couple of hoods who were stabbing him with the jagged shards of a broken bottle. His face was already covered in blood, and the hands he used to protect his face were already badly cut and bleeding. I thought, 'if someone doesn't do something soon, this chap could be cut to pieces'. I looked up and down the street. No one else was around. I knew it was up to me to do something but, I must confess, I was tempted to just walk on by – to pretend that I hadn't seen anything warranting my attention, let alone my intervention.

I was afraid, terribly afraid, and my fear was well-founded. It had a strong basis in fact. There were two men across the road trying to kill someone, and if I tried to help him chances were that I could be killed too. After all, there were two of them and only one of me. They looked like street fighters – and I looked like the wimp that I was. I had no weapon and wouldn't know how to use one even if I had one; and they had shards of sharp glass that they wielded as wickedly as the grim reaper himself might have swung his scythe.

I believe fear such as this should not be dismissed, because fears based in fact serve as a basic reality test for our intentions. Believe it or not, on a number of occasions when he was confronted by people who wanted to kill him, even Christ decided that it was better for him to run away and fight another day than to die for nothing at all (e.g.,

Luke 4:29-30). And sometimes it might be better for us to run away, too - the faster the better.

However, this was not one of those times. This time someone's life was at stake. Christ would not have run away on this occasion. And neither - really - could I. So I wrapped the tattered rags of my makeshift courage around me and, with trembling hands, wobbly knees, and a heart ringing like an alarm bell, I crossed the road to intervene in the fight.

I didn't rush over and try to crash tackle the assailants. That only ever works in the movies. And even then it doesn't work all the time. I simply walked to within ten metres of the mêlée, stopped, and said the most inoffensive thing I could think of at the time, which was 'G'day.'

The antagonists immediately turned in my direction. Now that I had their attention I tried to distract them from further hurting their victim. But the trick was to do it without them harming me instead. So I said to them, in as friendly a tone as I could muster, 'Can I help you?'

The aggressors looked at one another, then at me, and laughed. They thought it was a big joke. 'Does it look like we need any help?' they asked facetiously.

'No,' I said very carefully. 'It doesn't look like you need any help. But it looks like he might need some help. What d'you reckon?'

By now they had stopped stabbing their prey and, in answer to my question, they shrugged their shoulders and said, 'Well you help him then!'

And with that they walked off and left me to care for the mutilated man on the side of the road. He was seriously injured, but at least he was still alive. And so was I.

• • •

After World War II my father became a Christian. After becoming a Christian, he decided to become a pastor. And he spent much of his time as a pastor intervening in fights and mediating conflict resolution. So I grew up with an understanding that intervention was not enough. I learned that, wherever possible, it was important to move from intervention to mediation.

Ange and I once had a set of neighbours who had been feuding with each other for ten years. The problem was that the bloke we'll call Ben had some banana trees growing in his backyard that cast a shadow across his neighbour Bill's prize vegetable patch. And the bloke we'll call Bill used to mow his lawn at seven o'clock on a Sunday morning when Ben was trying to sleep off his hangover. As a result of this unresolved conflict, Ben and Bill hadn't talked to each other at all for the ten years before we moved in next door to them. Each morning I'd get up, go into my backyard, see them working in their gardens side by side, and say, 'G'day Ben! G'day Bill!' And both of them would look up, carefully so as avoid any eye contact, say 'G'day Dave!' to me and totally ignore the bloke standing next to them. They wouldn't even give one another the time of day.

Many times, Ange and I talked with them individually about resolving the conflict – but neither of them would budge. Then, one day, we heard the sounds of fighting – some swearing, pushing, and shoving – that ended ominously with a loud thump. After a few moments of silence, someone screamed, 'Bill's killed Ben!'

By the time we got there it was all over. Bill was hanging over the fence, breathlessly, staring at Ben, who was sprawled in a heap on the ground. We ran to see if Ben was still alive. He was knocked out cold but would live to fight another day. So we carried him upstairs and laid him on his bed to recover.

When he eventually came round I said to him, 'Listen, mate, you could have been killed today – all because you don't want to shift your banana trees. You've got to sort it out. Next time you may not be so lucky.'

Ben looked at me and smiled.

So I said, 'Be at my place tomorrow at three for a cup of tea and we'll try to sort it out.'

He nodded.

Then we jumped the fence over to Bill's place. He was sitting at the kitchen table with his wife, who was chastising him in no uncertain terms. When she'd finished with him I asked if I could say something. She was glad to have someone else have a go at him. And he was glad to see someone else, anyone besides her, to give him a break from the fury of her anger.

So I said to him, 'Bill, you could have killed someone today – all because you want to mow the lawn at seven o'clock on a Sunday morning. You've got to sort it out. Next time you could be in big trouble. They'll toss you in jail and throw away the key.'

Bill looked at me and grimaced.

So I said, 'Be at my place tomorrow at three for a cup of tea and we'll try to sort it out.'

He nodded.

The next day at three, bang on time, Ben and Bill turned up. I invited them in and they sat down, looking about rather shamefacedly. As I gave them cups of tea, I caught their eyes and asked, 'Well, what are we going to do?'

They said nothing. They both shrugged their shoulders and sat staring back at me.

'Well,' I said. 'It seems to me that we've got to try to end this feud before it's the end of us.'

'Yeah,' they both said, looking at each other for the first time in I don't know how long.

'What do you think you can do about it, Ben?' I asked.

'I could cut down my banana trees after the next bunches ripen and replant them further away from the fence,' Ben said.

'What do you think of that, Bill?' I asked.

'That's all I want,' said Bill.

'What do you think you can do in return, Bill?' I asked.

'I guess I could mow the lawn a bit later.'

'How much later?' I asked.

'Two hours later,' he said.

'What do you think of that, Ben?'

'That'll do me,' said Ben.

'Well, I reckon we might be pretty close to a deal here. What do you reckon?'

'Sure thing!' they replied, looking pretty pleased with themselves.

'Then I've just got two final questions,' I said.

'Shoot!' someone said – an unfortunate turn of phrase.

'First question is, what are you going to do next time one or other of you comes home drunk?'

Ben said, 'We don't have to hang over the fence and abuse each other. We can go to bed and sleep it off . . . as long as people let us sleep it off, that is.'

'What do you think of that, Bill?' I asked.

'Fine by me,' he said.

'So you're both happy with that?'

They nodded.

'Second question is, what if something comes up – what if you get into a bit of a scrap – what are you going to do then?'

Quick as a flash, Bill said, 'No worries! We'll just come over here, have a cup of tea, and sort it out!'

'What do you think of that, Ben?' I asked.

'Fine by me,' he said.

And, from that day on, they did exactly what they said they'd do. There were no more fights. After they bore the next bunches, the banana trees were cut down. The lawn still got mown regularly on a Sunday - but later, much later, in the day. In fact, the only sounds I ever heard early on Sunday mornings from then on were the sounds of Ben and Bill swapping handy hints with one another about their gardens as they went about their work side by side.

It was a touch of heaven on earth.

I believe that, in order to be the change I want to see in the world, I need to work for peace in any and every way I can. I believe I should intervene in violent situations wherever I can and mediate conflict resolution whenever I can. Wherever I intervene I need to proceed carefully, using my fear to test the level of risk and then – if I think there is a real possibility I can help in the situation – to proceed slowly but surely, addressing the perpetrators, distracting their attention, diffusing their aggression, and negotiating entry to provide aid for the victim.

Whenever I mediate I need to proceed carefully, connecting with the people who are in dispute and approaching these antagonists as potential allies. I need to establish, or re-establish, communication between the parties to the dispute. I need to try to help both sides understand one another, clear up any misunderstandings, enable both sides to relate as fellow human beings, negotiate a deal between the parties in the dispute, and broker an arrangement acceptable to all – always being mindful of the fact that without justice there can be no peace.

8

**We can be people
who cope with flack**
and see the
difference it makes
to the way we can
incarnate enduring,
ongoing change.

Nowhere in the Gospels does Jesus ever suggest that suffering – especially suffering persecution – is essentially meritorious or glorious. What Jesus does say is this: 'Blessed are those who are persecuted because of righteousness' (Matt. 5:10). It is the willingness to suffer persecution 'because of righteousness' which is inherently worthwhile.

· · ·

When most Christians talk about persecution they are referring to persecution by non-Christians – like the Hindu militants who have burned down two hundred churches in Orissa as I write. But my experience of persecution has been predominantly at the hands of fellow Christians – because I criticize Christians for preaching about Christ but not practicing the radical, inclusive, non-violent compassion of Christ. The irony is that when they attack me for pointing this out, it only proves my point.

I have never been persecuted to the extent that someone has tried to 'put me to death' (Matt. 10:21) – although some people, in a deliberate, orchestrated attempt to destroy me, have threatened to kill me, and others have 'insulted' me and said 'falsely all kinds of evil' against me (Matt. 5:11). I have also been scolded, censured, and sacked. I've been dressed down, beaten up, and tossed out on the street. I've been officially excommunicated and formally ostracized. As a result, people like Gordon Preece, the editor of *Zadok Perspectives*, publicly refer to me as a 'Jeremiah' – 'a weeping prophet'. And they may be right.

· · ·

In the build-up to the war on Iraq, I was alarmed by the way the media in Australia were demonizing Muslims. As we all know, demonizing people is always just an excuse to destroy them. So I went to the local mosque and said, 'Christians, Muslims, and Jews all believe that Abraham is the father of our faith, and we all believe our God is the God of Abraham. So, rather than let the press play us off against each other, why don't we show our unity by coming together for prayer? And to start that process, why don't I come and pray with you at the mosque on Friday?'

'Sure,' they said. So I did. But to judge by the reaction of some Christians to my praying with my Muslim friends, you'd think that I'd sold my soul to the devil.

When war was declared, I wrote an open letter to our troops.

An Open Letter to Our Troops

Aussies have always been proud of our diggers. And no nation could have been prouder of their troops than when the ADF went to the aid of the people of East Timor. But this war does not have the support of the UN, the world community, or the majority of the Australian people. Why? Not even the CIA can make a link between Al Qaeda and Iraq. Sure, Saddam is a butcher. But killing more innocent Iraqis is no solution. We are told Iraq has weapons of mass destruction. But so does Israel. And no one is saying we should invade Israel. Most of the world sees this war as immoral, illegal, and ill-advised. It is US aggression, in contravention of the UN, that will only serve to create more ill will – even if it succeeds in regime change.

We therefore beg you, in the great Aussie tradition, to disobey all orders that defy common sense and common decency – and refuse to fight in this war. We will, of course, support you as people whatever you decide to do.

Yours sincerely,

Dave Andrews,
An Aussie for an Honourable Australia[16]

As you can imagine, Christians who believe we should always 'submit ourselves to the governing authorities' (regardless of whether they are right or wrong) because there is 'no authority except that which God has established' (Rom. 13:1), considered my call for the troops to disobey their orders tantamount to blasphemy.

They fixated on the verse but forgot to interpret the verse in context. They forgot that what Paul wrote in Romans 13 was meant to be interpreted in the context of Romans 12, and that Paul began Romans 12 with his great revolutionary cry: 'Do not conform any longer to the pattern of this world, but be transformed by the renewing of your mind . . . then (and only then) you will be able to test and approve what God's will is – his good, pleasing and perfect will' (Rom. 12:2). When I reminded them that 'Peter and the other apostles' made the same point – that when it came to a conflict between obeying God and obeying men 'We must obey God rather than men [sic]!'

(Acts 5:29) – some of my detractors were as furious at me as the crowd was at Peter when he first said these words.

• • •

When the coalition troops marched triumphantly into Baghdad, one pastor in a church on the Sunshine Coast just north of where I live actually stopped in the middle of the service to lead his congregation in three cheers for the victory. When I heard about that, I resolved to myself that the next chance I got to speak at a church in the Sunshine State I would directly address the issue of the war in Iraq. So when a friend of mine who was a pastor asked me to preach at his church on Isaiah 2:3-4 I thought it was an answer to prayer.

The famous words in Isaiah 2:3-4 portray a beautiful vision of God's call for us to make peace.

> 'Come,
> let us go up to the mountain of the LORD,
> to the house of the God of Jacob.
> He will teach us his ways,
> so that we may walk in his paths.'
> The law will go out from Zion,
> the word of the LORD from Jerusalem.
> He will judge between the nations
> and will settle disputes for many peoples.
> They will beat their swords into plowshares
> and their spears into pruning hooks.
> Nation will not take up sword against nation,
> nor will they train for war anymore.
>
> (Isaiah 2:3-4)

So I got up in the pulpit and began to review America's foreign policy and Australia's foreign policy in the light of God's foreign policy outlined in this text. You might think good Bible-believing Christians would be happy to engage contemporary issues from a scriptural perspective. But they got very upset. One person stood up and strode out of the church. Then another. And another. Then two or three more people decided it was time to go. Soon, whole rows of people were streaming out of their pews down the aisle towards the door.

I didn't know what to do. But I knew that if I didn't do something I'd lose the whole congregation. So I said that if people disagreed with me and wanted to leave as a protest against what I was saying that was okay by me. But, I said, if they chose to stay I wouldn't take it as a sign that they agreed with me – only as a sign that they were prepared to listen to another point of view respectfully, regardless of whether they agreed with it or not.

As I said this people stopped and looked at one another, wondering what they should do. A few still decided to leave. But many decided to stay. In the end, probably a third of the congregation ended up walking out. And of the two-thirds who stayed, not a single person from the church was willing to talk to me. One person did eventually come over to talk to me, but she turned out to be a visitor.

When my friend, the pastor who had invited me to speak, returned from leading the kids' talk, which was on at the same time as the sermon, he took one look at the disaster and told me that as much as he loved me he was afraid he would never be able to invite me back to speak at his church again.

• • •

While the war has continued I have carried on working on dialogue between Christians and Muslims, trying to rebuild the relational bridges between our communities that the propaganda in the media blows up on the front pages of our newspapers every day. The Ramadan before last we organized an *iftar* (a meal to break the fast) with fifty Christians and fifty Muslims. We started with prayer then ate lightly spiced *halal* food and drank bright sparkling non-alcoholic drinks while some great local musicians played wonderful Middle Eastern folk songs in the background. Mixed groups of Christians and Muslims sat around the tables and chatted about their lives, their faith, and their values, celebrating their similarities and discussing their differences in a beautifully respectful manner.

Last Ramadan we decided that, rather than have a meal together, we would provide a meal together for marginalized and disadvantaged people in our city. Some of us have been hosting a regular shared meal with people who live on the streets or in hostels or some of the boarding houses in our neighbourhood for more than twenty years. So we invited our Christian and Muslim friends to join us. Our Muslim friends offered to serve the food, which they did. Then they moved out from behind the safety of the serving counters to sit and eat with the people they had served – who at times, I must admit, seem a bit scary.

One of the great moments for me in those times that we had together at the community meal was to see a young Muslim woman wearing a *hijab* – with whom I had deliberately not shaken hands when introduced to her – graciously returning the innocent embrace of a man with an intellectual disability who had spontaneously reached out and wrapped her in his arms in gratitude.

However, on three occasions recently when I have tried to share my experiences working with Muslims, some Christians I was speaking to got very angry with me. It is as if I'm a traitor, as if I'm letting the side down. In encouraging Christians to let down their guard, I am betraying Christendom by giving Muslims the chance to take over our country when we are off guard.

When I respond by saying that in the past thousand years there have been more devastating wars among so-called Christian states fighting each other than between Christian and Muslim states, they don't want to hear it. And when I tell them that predominantly 'Christian' states have killed more Jews and Muslims than predominantly Muslim states have killed Christians or Jews,[17] they tend to get even angrier.

In my experience, there is nothing that makes Christians angrier than to suggest that everything good you can find in Christianity you can find in other religions, and that everything bad you can find in other religions you can find in Christianity – and that it is Jesus, not Christianity as a religion, that is the good news.

• • •

I used to teach a course on Christian community work at a Christian College in Queensland. At the start of the course, I always asked students to draw a picture of their ideal community. Not surprisingly, many of these Christian students drew pictures of Christian communities with churches with steeples and crosses at the centres.

'So your ideal community is a Christian community,' I would observe.

'Yes,' they would say. 'It is.'

'So where is the place in your ideal community for people who are not Christians?' I would ask.

'In our ideal community everyone is a Christian,' they would say proudly.

'So,' I would say to them, 'if everyone in your ideal community is a Christian, and you want to work to make this ideal a reality, then the only options for Muslims in your world would be for them to be converted – or terminated. And that is exactly the same aggressive, intolerant attitude that Christians accuse Muslims of advocating. Where is the good news of Jesus in that?'

Someone made a complaint to the faculty about the kinds of things I was saying in my course about Christianity as a religion. An inquiry was held, which included a lecturer in theology who had been the best man at my wedding and who had gone off to do his PhD at Dallas when Ange and I had gone off to work in Delhi. Though I thought that I acquitted myself quite well at the inquiry, after it was over

I was never invited back to teach another course at the college until more than ten years later when my friend, the lecturer in theology, finally retired.

• • •

Over the years I have been banned, barred, and black-listed, excluded, expelled, and excommunicated from many Christian groups and organizations. The challenge for me has always been to absorb the evil without 'returning evil for evil' and escalating the cycle of violence in the world (Rom. 12:17).

I agree with Gale Webb, who says that 'there are many ways to deal with evil. All of them are facets of the truth that the only ultimate way to conquer evil is to let it be smothered within a willing, living, human being. When it is absorbed there, like a spear into one's heart, it loses its power and goes no further.' Those who 'turn the other cheek' when they are persecuted for righteousness, as Christ said, are blessed because when they absorb the insult and the injury 'like a spear into one's heart' the evil 'goes no further'.[18]

So over the years I have absorbed the evil and looked for opportunities to 'return good for the evil' done to me (Rom. 12: 21). And, as a result, in the last ten years I have been able to reconcile with every single Christian institution who rejected me - including the church that said they would never have me back!

I believe that in order to be the change I want to see in the world I need to cope with the flack involved in advocating change. I believe that, in an evil world, I will only ever be free to do good if I am prepared to suffer persecution. It is in my willingness to suffer that I have freedom to act. I believe that to be persecuted for doing good is evil. When people do evil to me, the temptation is for me to return evil for evil. But that only strengthens the stranglehold evil has on the world. So, instead of reacting to evil, I know I need to absorb evil, without reacting to it, and thus destroy its power. I believe that my suffering can reflect the way of Christ – the only beacon of hope for compassion in the dark corners of our world.

I believe that if I were to get through life without scars, the big question I would have to answer would be: 'Was there nothing you felt was worth fighting for?'

We can be people who are with the poor in spirit and who see the difference it makes to the way we locate ourselves in the world.

We can be people who weep with those who weep, and we can see the difference it makes to the way we can relate to the world.

We can be people who are meek, angry yet restrained, and see the difference it makes to the way we can respond to the world.

We can be people who seek to do right by others, and see the difference it makes to the way that we can engage our world.

We can be people who seek to do right by others and see the difference it makes to the way that we can engage our world.

We can be people who act with integrity and see the difference that it makes to the way that we can activate true change.

We can be people who work for peace and see the difference that it makes to the way that we can actuate non-violent change.

We can be people who cope with flack and see the difference it makes to the way we can incarnate enduring, ongoing change.

The Plan Be Pledge

I Want to Be the Change I Want to See . . .

I will identify with the poor in spirit.

I will grieve over injustice in the world.

I will get angry, but never get aggressive.

I will seek to do justice, even to my enemies.

I will extend compassion to all those in need.

I will act with integrity, not for the publicity.

I will work for peace in the midst of violence.

I will suffer myself, rather than inflict suffering.

Signed.....................................Date.............

Warning:
We need to take the Be-Attitudes seriously,
but we shouldn't take ourselves too seriously.

Check out the www.wecan.be website.

Notes

1 E. Wiesel, *Night* (New York: Hill and Wang, 1960), p. 70.

2 J. Attalli, *Millennium* (New York: Random House, 1991), p. 84.

3 Attalli, *Millennium*, pp. 73-74.

4 K. Miller, 'Six Billion to Feed', *The Courier Mail* (22 Sept. 1999), p. 19.

5 *The Burden of Debt Jubilee 2000 Coalition* (Melbourne, 1999), p. 3.

6 *The Jubilee 2000 Debt Cutter's Handbook* (London, 1998), p. 13.

7 Eknath Easwaran, *A Man to Match his Mountains* (Petaluma: Nilgiri Press, 1984), p. 63.

8 Easwaran, *A Man to Match his Mountains*, foreword.

9 Easwaran, *A Man to Match his Mountains*, pp. 88-89.

10 Easwaran, *A Man to Match his Mountains*, pp. 117, 209.

11 Easwaran, *A Man to Match his Mountains*, pp. 110-12.

12 Easwaran, *A Man to Match his Mountains*, p. 113.

13 Easwaran, *A Man to Match his Mountains* pp. 122-24.

14 Shrinivas Rao Sohoni, 'Badshah Khan: Islam and Non-Violence', in *Khan Abdul Ghaffar Khan: A Centennial Tribute* (New Delhi: Har-Anand Publications, 1995), p. 48.

15 Kushwant Singh, *Delhi: A Novel* (Delhi: Sangham Books, 1983), pp. 4-5.

16 In case you're wondering what I think we should have done, I think we should have done everything we could have done ethically to undermine Saddam's regime short of invading his country. We didn't need to invade the Soviet Union to bring down the wall. And we didn't need to invade South Africa to put an end to apartheid. But we did need to actively support the efforts of genuine dissidents.

17 'Alive and Kicking', *New Internationalist* (Aug. 2004).

18 G. Webbe, *The Night and Nothing* (New York: Seabury Press, 1964), p. 109.